This book belongs to

....

This is the story of Jonah the Moaner.

You can read it with others, or read it alone-a.

It does have a few long words like Nineveh,

But give it a go, even if you're a beginniver!

(We made that word up.)

One thing more – can you guess what?

On every page there are some sunglasses to spot!

Jonah
the
Moaner

Nick and Claire Page

Illustrations by Nikki Loy

make
believe
ideas

Once there was a city full of lies and hate,
With great big walls and a great big gate.
Its people were rich and mean and strong,
But God didn't like it when they did wrong.

(It was called Nineveh.)

So God called a man from a faraway land
To tell them their city would turn to sand.
They had to say "sorry" in the next forty days,
They had to change their minds and their
nasty ways.

(The man was
called Jonah.)

Jonah had heard about nasty Nineveh,
So God's command put him in a spinniver.
"I can't go there, because I'll end up dead,
I think I'll take a trip to sunny Spain instead!"

(So he went
to Tarshish.)

So he packed his case
with a ticket for Tarshish,
Took a bucket and a spade
to look for starfish.

But out at sea, a storm
began to brew...
The captain was scared
and his crew were too!
(They were wet as well.)

And where was Jonah?
He was snoozing downstairs!
"Get up," cried the captain,
"and say your prayers!
It's all your fault that this
ship's going down.
If you don't own up we're
all going to drown!"

(Poor old Jonah!)

"You're right," said Jonah.
"I'm running away.
Throw me off the boat and you'll be OK!"
So the sailors picked him up
and they threw him in the sea;
The waves died down – and they all had tea.
(Except for Jonah.)

Deep in the ocean it was teatime too,
And a REALLY BIG FISH
wanted something to chew.
With a flick of its tail
and a Chomp Chomp Slurp,
It swallowed up Jonah:
Chomp Chomp Burp!

(It was a REALLY
BIG FISH, you see.)

16

Then God said:
"Jonah the Moaner,
don't be a groaner!
Look where it's got you –
all wet and alone-a!
You can't run away
to the starfish in Tarshish.
Just do what I say,
double-quick!
Make it sharpish!"

"Sorry, God," said Jonah,
as he wobbled in the belly.
"I'll do what you want!
Get me out and quick – it's smelly!"

So God sent the fish
to a beach real quick,
And the REALLY BIG FISH
brought up Jonah in his sick!

(Which was NOT very nice.)

19

God told Jonah as he hit dry land:
"Go and tell those nasty Ninnies
they'll be turned to sand.
If they don't change their ways
in the next few weeks,
There'll be a-crashing and a-smashing
and shouts and shrieks."

(And he
meant it.)

So Jonah went and told them,
and to his surprise,
They decided to be good –
there were tears in their eyes!
The king told Jonah,
"Thanks for bringing this from God,
Now go away please –
you really smell of cod."

(Which is a
kind of fish.)

So God forgave the Ninnies,
but it made Jonah mad!
He just let them off –
and they'd been so bad!
It didn't make sense,
Jonah just couldn't see.
He said, "There's something fishy here,
if you ask me."

(Jonah was
a moaner.)

22

And God said:
"Jonah the Moaner,
don't be a groaner!
I am in charge,
from here to Arizona.
I forgive them if they're sorry,
every day, that's my way.
Take it easy, don't worry –
you can have a holiday."

"Jonah the Moaner,
your work here is through.
The starfish in Tarshish
Are waiting for you!"

Ready to tell

Oh no! Some of the pictures from this story have been mixed up! Can you retell the story and point to each picture in the correct order?

Picture dictionary

Encourage your child to read these harder words from the story and gradually develop their basic vocabulary.

alone

beach

city

holiday

scared

snooze

starfish

storm

wave

Key words

Here are some key words used in context. Help your child to use other words from the border in simple sentences.

Jonah ran **away**.

A **big** fish swallowed him.

"**I** am sorry," he said.

He **went** to the city.

Everyone **was** sorry.

Make a Jonah jello!

Here's how to recreate a scene from this story.
It's fun to do – and to eat!

You will need

a packet of green jello • fondant icing (in lots of colors)
• one or two ladyfingers • a mixing jug or bowl
• a large spoon • a large glass bowl

What to do

1 Make the jello in a mixing bowl or jug, following the instructions on the packet. (Ask a grown-up to help you.) When the jello has cooled, put it in the fridge to set.

2 Use the icing to model a ship, a big fish and Jonah. Put these to one side to dry out.

3 Use more icing to make fish, other underwater creatures and wavy seaweed.

4 Press the underwater shapes to the inside of the glass bowl. A drop of water may help them stick.

5 Sprinkle some crumbled ladyfingers onto the bottom of the bowl to make "sand."

6 When the jello has set, stir and chop it into tiny pieces. Carefully spoon it into the glass bowl.

7 On top of the jello, make a scene with the ship, the big fish and Jonah. Serve immediately.